SORTING IT OUT

SORTING IT OUT

poems by
Anne S. Perlman

Carnegie-Mellon University Press
Pittsburgh 1982
Feffer and Simons, Inc., London

811

P422a

ACKNOWLEDGMENTS

Poems in this collection have been published in the following magazines:

The Nation: "The Wonderful Stereopticon Machine", "Continuum", "Is this it?", "From the Headland", "Keep Still", "Survival", "Viking 1 on Mars— July 20, 1976", "The Specialist", "Summer Hillside", *The Hudson Review*: "Summer Adjustments", "Poem for a Cousin", "Easter Snow", *Response*: "Messages (For Nelly Sachs and Anna Akhmatova)", *Mademoiselle*: "Baleen", "Shelter", *Poetry Now*: "To the Tel Aviv Antique Dealer", "What Counted", *West Coast Poetry Review*: "Running the Rapids", *The Paris Review*: "Family Reunion", *Occident*: "Childbirth", *Intro #1* (anthology, Bantam, 1968): "Suicide", *Padan Aram*: "Suicide", *Poets West* (anthology, Perivale Press, 1976): "Childbirth", *Sidelines*: "Selling off the Garden", *Berkeley Poets' Cooperative*: "Back to Tijuana". *Ploughshares*: "Aliens on Exmoor", *California Living*: "House-Dweller", "Sharers", "Family Reunion", "Continuum", "What Counted", "From the Headland", *California Quarterly*: "A Dying", "At the Houghton Library", *The Southern Review*: "A Housewife Riddle", "The Moray", *Planned Parenthood Review*: "Back to Tijuana", *The Three Rivers Poetry Journal*: "Search", "At Fifty in the Crystal-Dead Eye of the Center", *Science 81*: "At Liberty".

The publication of this book is supported by grants from the National Endowment for the Arts in Washington, D.C., a Federal agency, and from the Pennsylvania Council on the Arts.

Library of Congress Catalog Card Number 82-70744
ISBN 0-915604-72-8
ISBN 0-915604-73-6 pbk.
Copyright © 1982 by Anne S. Perlman
Printed and bound in the United States of America
First Edition

115741

CONTENTS

I

II

III

IV

For David

I

SURVIVAL

This love
is our own mix . . .
a given,
like the rose I find
in a rough fall of pine cones . . .
or a single kite spool
here in our hands,
its twine unwinding
up the drafts
over light settling
red on an iron mountain.
And on toward the harshness of stars
rounding the sky.

It is this knowing
I have a stubborn
glittering ally . . .
who will vouch
I passed this way.

FAMILY REUNION

All right. Let's hear it
for this fine figure of a
trout on every plate.
In front of me on white china
his fry-dark belly
dark as my own bones,
closet bones
that will never see light.

Now then,
cut off his head.
The quick guillotine
at the quieting table.
Slit the thin skin,
lay back two neat
sections of flesh,
the vertebrae intact.
There'll be no thrust and parry
of his bones darting in my throat.

Flip the body
to repeat on his underside.
The spine lifts out easily.
White how white
its bones are.
Do I have any part
of me left,
whole and shiny?
These secret fish bones
have no cracks.

Against the brittle talk
breaking up the table,
I lay that trout's
perfectly branching core
by its blind head
at the rim of my plate.

RUNNING THE RAPIDS

Edging the cliffs,
remnants of lava boil
into griffins and unicorns,
thrusting at aurochs
and mongol horses.
They crouch over us,
grow fierce in the wind
as branches batter
their open mouths.
Water and sun slash
wet light in their eyes.
Echoes from rapids
down the gorge
howl through their stony lips
until the hoofs and the mouths
burst free.

This river is cold as a dinosaur.
A traveler could go mad.

Then from narrow ice pools
a rush of jaws:
but where are the whales
in the larger creeks of the ocean?

At night we shall lie together
warm on a shelf of gravel,
narrow below first cliffs,
watching the alders touch stars.

THE MORAY

Five squat men
with a five-pronged spear,
home from a night
on coral reefs,
bend a lantern
over the long corpse.
Reef-foam
lights its nostrils.
The eyes are ocean holes.

Inside, the paralyzing venom stirs.

As we peer across the sand,
strolling in night clothes
down the stone steps of our lanai,
the fishermen spring upright
to screen their capital prize.
They link themselves
into a round of backs,
muscles swollen against strangers.
Slowly they circle that knobby one
who kills after his own death.

SUMMER HILLSIDE

Chasing uphill
catching at the wind for breath
we move jointless as
erratic ghosts   become
part of the wild rye . . .
these great white whorls
bending and rearing
in the green mane . . . become
a part of the lather
a part of the green.

                Once-removed now
from our very selves,
a cranky sense of omen comes.
Our reflections in a flat
of spring water look foreign.
Our arms too shiny
in the late sunlight.

Suddenly, the wind is turning fierce,
harsh as a firehose,
loosens the roots of the grasses,
flails at our summer clothing.
Maims our own shadows.

Shielded only by dread
against this seedless quickening,
we stand upright and nameless
on the open hillside,
rooted spare as lightning poles
to ground the swelling roar.

SUICIDE

On this day you are dying
I have a faceful of bees,
a rag of chloroform across
my nose and mouth.
Caterpillars slide on my arm.

We shall inherit the strangling cloth,
your death by your hand.

Even if you can't scoop pain
from the fragile body,
shouldn't the cross-grained
mind still live out its days,
numbered by a recording angel
whose eye alone matters? Or
North cannot be chained in space.

Now, you unlock the gate,
and on two frail legs, you
are walking through the wall.
I hear you in my mind. Not waiting
for rhythmic chance
on a day for loving.

Things. The dog a crackle
of soupbones on our porch.
Candyjars and tureen
poised and round on this day
light is wasting from edges.
There is a streaming, falling.
Clouds uncouple from a charging sky.

THE NEWS

glides above
our frozen meadow
and nothing changes.

In the cabin we listen
by crystal or satellite.
We only flinch.
Out of our range
the numbers defeat us,
remain apart and sinewy.
A blackrobed myth.

Only the static . . .
that appalling hum in numbers
of hunger and overkill . . .
only the static gets through.

SHELTER

I see you through
blue motes, occupying
your own space. Light
fills the space between us.
I take no room.

Your ears slant a little
to water sliding
on kelp, and you
breathe the salt. Skin
moulded tight on
your strong nose.
Where I want to melt,
your neck is strong and young
holding intact a head of arrows.
You live in your tight skin.

But your eyes drive toward
me, who fills no space.
Your arms pull me into
a room where I am warm. Roofed.

A DYING

Such a meticulous traveler,
how can you go
with no baggage
                              no map?

Meager as loose barnacles,
we poke the edges of water,
pick up rocks
and clumps of seaweed;
driftwood to make ourselves bulky.

We listen for you in sea shells,
see your face a disorder of waves,
your breath held close.
And now the only sounds
are your fingers straightening
into little sticks.

CHILDBIRTH

Comment va-t-elle, Docteur?
Elle est parfaite, Madame.

The distant words
swallowed by my foreign ear.

After pain,
this haze . . . this dazzle?

They say I will forget labor.

* * *

It is February now,
and we are chilled
in the cafe until
the winter sun bursts
hotter than August
over the table.
My gloomy wine glass
quickens in the new light,
glistens, casts a shadow,
like the map in myself
filled with common boundaries.
Between my light
and my darkness . . .
those necessary neighbors.

If one of them left,
I would lose myself
in my own house.

II

BALEEN

Baleen from a rotting whale, and slipper
shells, slide out of your hands. Float
about our glide into the ocean's
heavy light. Water overlapping in the round;
we are a being.

Laid flat in crests breaking,
I have rock feelings. Erosion.
The water soothes my thighs as I
thin into clouds. My name is gone.

I am part of a disdainful cloud,
yet the stunted pitchpine is my dream
of growing. The tide pulls me
from shallows, gives me moonstrength.
I want no seasonal adjustments, only
the immediate season from here to there.
No thing. I want to be no thing.

Only movement toward you, with you:
to be a sea bass, sea gull, sea anemone.
A piece of movement, flow of movement.
To be the light! Before the word,
before dust, before the mollusk that inhabited
the slipper shell. Before the rotting whale.

BACK TO TIJUANA

Abortion Foes Now
Claim Huge Support
San Francisco Chronicle

The Tijuana abortionist is waiting.
He is smiling with eyes like spoons.
His breath hums: a vacuum cleaner.
The treatment room is ready.

While he waits for
the fresh blackmarket,
he croons over his rags and mops
that could clean up
a stockyard,
a tide wrack . . .
any havoc.

His close-coupled body
is strong enough to carry
these large-boned
gringo women into his recovery room.
Place them on cots
and smile.

A knightly smile
that comes with winning a joust,
slaying the dragon,
emptying the courtyard of invaders.
He is a true-blue Macho Papa,
father of twelve legitimate children
in his off-hours.
He can afford to smile
at the empty vessels
he has unloaded,
peering into their bobbing past.
He is a grateful parishioner.

A HOUSEWIFE RIDDLE

She keeps a covey of quail
under her arms,
sandpipers to her breasts.
Walking waist-high in ponds
she can swim among lilypads
without strangling.

Frail reader of the news,
her smile is fragile
as her skin. She cries
as quickly as she bleeds.
Her head is crowded with
milkwort and flimsies.

POEM FOR A COUSIN

We rested lightly against you
for safe passage,
a river rock to cross from here to there.

This loss is too swift,
a dream cat
sliding over my doorsill.

If only we could recite
our tales of dread and disaster
(always with miraculous endings).
Familiar, permanent.

You were this family's vault of legends.
We knew the comfort of kinswomen,
flowing across our clannish field . . .
It was the stuff of our lives.

EASTER SNOW

Too fat, too brief, too late.
These flakes slanting
out of season.

No joy here
like Indian Summer
with its warmth . . .
that last cast of light
on our walls, in our bones.

FROM THE HEADLAND

Barefoot from the headland,
back along the beach
past sand dollars,
homeless,
their lives half under sky
half under water . . .
they glitter
black lights at the flood.
Radios watches glasses
go out with the old sand
and children will ride
canoes on the new water.

AN OLD CONCERN FOR TERRITORY

She sees her boy
in the pasture.
Oh, he is safe out there
from mortal talk.
Flanked by lambs
who merely know of life.
Only an old concern for territory calls.

They are at ease
boy and lambs,
away from talk . . .
away
from words pouring like infertile eggs,
words lying like fruit forks in rotting plums,
words with the terrible knowledge of seeds.

In silence she turns back to the house.

THE SPECIALIST

He no longer marvels at stars.
That's what.

Under the telescope's dome,
he crouches in a
concrete basement,
his head down,
decoding the graphs
a cosmic camera
drops in his lap.

In his own regional head
(it could be a dungeon)
he parses electrical impulses,
regroups the lines
(fudging a little)
into lakes and sandstorms,
peaks and tide wracks,
his whole territory
shut against trespassers.

AT THE HOUGHTON LIBRARY

(For Emily Dickinson)

                    Frightened
in your father's gardens
by the wind and light,
yourself the center
of circumference
eye of your own typhoon,

how you hide
from callers
as Adam hid! . . .
Ajar with bony wonder
inside your sockets,
can you find love
scrabbling for eternity
in cookie tins?

In heat so fierce
it burns away the walls?

MESSAGES

(For Nelly Sachs and Anna Akhmatova)

Poems from these northern women
bereft in their fullness,
left over from purges and ovens,
drive spikes in my eyes.

Our southern mornings turn heavy as night,
the beach thin and hot
a confusion of fins and wings,
sunbathers hollow in their oiled skins.
Umbrellas all the umbrellas are broken.

The parched voices of these women
chosen to record
towns of horror . . .
their cries skim over the poles.
Against our sand cliff
I hear the wind split,
and then the dead weight.

TO THE TEL AVIV ANTIQUE DEALER

We fill the jug with water
and earth-smell saturates the room,
thirty-five hundred years of earth.
The walls tumbling down:
As I lean over your wet jug,
breathe from it, my dress changes
in a spinnery of generations.
Head covered, my body draped
with shawls and robes:
High on Jericho mud.
I want to chew it, breathe out,
to know even the overtaste of Jericho.

SEARCH

Do you hear those
iron wings scraping?
A rasp of crickets
hangs like sawteeth,
yet I hear it steadfast,
safe as wire screens
on my summer sleeping porch.

For ease I lean
to these other species.
Our neat partitions sag.
A prince would make a better frog,
I, a mare.

Can those crickets hear
the gait of my whisper,
its racking singlefoot?
I am what I am what?

THE WONDERFUL STEREOPTICON MACHINE

1

To grieve purely
in the garden
for the red bird
swallowed by a cat

      never looking at
      the cat's stomach
      in wonder . . .

      to know that instant
      for itself,
      only as the bird's
      the one who died early.

2

Gold on the cage grazes a golden
mechanical bird outside motionless

Close one eye here's the bird
close the other that barren cage
open both eyes wide to see
those wingy feathers under gold

But still the bird
framed only by his own gold feathers
unruffled silent
beak to the sky remains

alone . . . I will not cage him.

DANCE OF NINES

I hear you wore
your riding hat.
Like jumping gates
on Star. That terror.
This time you were alone.
Standing on a balcony.
I see you reciting
multiplication tables,
maybe the dance of nines.
Inexorable, this elegance
of numbers. Your ritual . . .
like the formality of manners
inside the logical game.
Steadying.
Nine times nine.

* * *

I know I know I know

I can't unscrew your pain
it's a tick in my side
a thousand ticks in my side.

One step at a time
that's the way we do . . .

Yourself standing
in the center
of a courtyard
horses blazing alone over gates
all else used up

doctors   lovers
saddlebags of pills
all used up
your body tilts from the center
no place   there's no place
inside anymore
only an elevator
up the well.
Past the walls.
You fall free.

KEEP STILL

very still
like a sundial,
logician of shadows.

Be silent as stiles,
stony to the hand,
under our vaulting bodies.

Or a fresh-water pond
secreting lily stems,
their noose around us.
Come, watch steam in a pot
build without sound,
hoarding its force
(only overgrown
it growls with cookery).

Soldiers and the sick
stifle their breathing.
The troops stiffen to sight down
the barrels of guns . . .
the sick chill on x-ray tables,
waiting for the foreign pictures.

Is stillness the first wonder?

We see the circus fellow on all fours
at the base of his human pyramid.
He will last.
He knows the quiet of sawdust.

III

SUMMER ADJUSTMENTS

1

Go softly now in the presence of circles,
along the low marsh roadway
between blackbirds and gulls:
in the sticky wind of the valley
wings are brushing.

2

Now we are passengers
bunched in a foreign train
compartment (no matter the country).
Our strangeness breaks over us,
crowded against
a man and a woman
in love. They are together
inside the circle of their shoulders.
It's the talk (no matter the language)
so close, so freighted
the circuit is closed.
Outside their brilliant territory
                              we dwindle.

3

Motionless in the August heat
we notice the shadow on the sundial,
how it curves through the weather.
Our heads turn to the sun's glare,
taste the heat wasting in our mouths.

WHAT COUNTED

(San Francisco)

What did count?
The kindness of fire engines
with ranks of profiles
in Napoleonic hats.
A trust in cobblers,
fishmongers, the iceman
and real-silk merchants . . .
A mistrust of riding masters,
lion tamers and nursemaids . . .
A confidence in streetcars and cablecars,
in the motorman
who let me reel the trolley,
in the gripman
who let me hook the cable.
A comfort in the hammers
of piano tuners and blacksmiths.
The feel of history
bolstering us with
news of the extinct:
like oracles and Great Auks . . .
I salute them all,
and they nod briskly
across my fancy,
busy at their tasks.

LAST TURN

Coasting fast in the dark,
our toboggan slides
under the turmoil of drafts
roiling high in Orion,

where winds roll and scrape
at the darkness of clouds . . .
until fresh stars show:
Young stars
bursting
in their hot litter
of brilliance.
New masters of light years,
they will glitter us quiet.

Here below, we stretch
in our own narrow instant;
the sky still familiar,
with the ridge line
its darker hem.
We are safe as a vaulted choir.
Singing carols,
we sweep down the frozen road.

PRAY FOR A RAINY DAY

If we must leave
these ample days
of sun and kindness,
we'll wait out the weather.
For rain fastening
the beach to the sky.
Only then,
we'll haul in
towels and snorkels,
our thermos and wicker hamper . . .

Swing our gear
through the bowels of thunder.

We can never leave
openly in sunlight,
warm with the smell of yarrow,
the taste of wild raspberries.
To watch our own shadows
breaking in the brilliant water
would bind us over
to this territory.
Emplaced for all seasons
like barnacle to oyster,
oyster to rock.

INLAND PASSAGE

To be the oldest
of them all
with nothing but sky
                overhead,
shrubs below
that never stood tall
in a high wind
with leaves, branches,
                trunk
listing listing
in waves of dust and soil
until the packed earth
rips, and the root-keel
is visible at last.

* * *

From the house,
they call to hurry.
Lunch, or tea, whatever.
Functions feel
like funerals now,
those omens of my own passage.
Through the rounding air
I hear again
their calls for ceremony.
I am too old to listen.

RELATIVES

This stone greying indoors
warms to our touch . . .
now it has no climate but our own.

Awash, it was porous
alive with iron
a slippery oval
greener than wet emeralds.

When we took it fresh
from a trough of pebbles
it was a green blaze in the hand
seizing a piece of the light.

We knew the roof waters
of darkness, creatures and rocks . . .
rocks and creatures . . .
broken equally against each other
by this impartial ocean.

ALIENS ON EXMOOR

Watch out for the lady riding sidesaddle!

On foot in the foreign gorse,
we watch the woman's private ride
thicken her with territory;
her figure is a jowl of land
rising against the sky.
If she comes near,
she will not confirm us.

She canters from the horizon
pasted to a rocking horse,
eyes hidden from the rain
under the brim of her bowler.
So it's true! Here,
we are nearly invisible.

Closer, she slows to a trot,
posting.
Only her own body exists,
the shielded head remote
from her center as toenails.

She will not bear witness.
We shrink level with the gorse.

Now the muffled one lowers
over the rim of her moor.
We take shape again,
grow tall through the heather,

our umbrella up against dangers.
We nod in unison knowing
something silent
as a thief or a mime,
intact as a dancer,
passed by.
We can hear our own breath.

CONTINUUM

Don't ask me where they went
jumping from sunny bridges
falling, falling.
My great-grandfather
looks correct
in his narrow album.
My father, too.

Do you see the iron sea horse
how it clangs? Carved in the
stone of its pedestal is my
father's name.
And I stumble
down the sunlit terrace
to that statue
knowing yes knowing
its passage
through whose hands it
passes to the campus grove.
Here the generations pat
the cold metallic back
listen to the echo . . .

I, too, will deny
the fine line celebrated
by funerals . . . my blood
runs thick and easy
under my thin skin.
I hear trees fall alone
in forests as my will
skirrs free through moonlight
on the backs of owls. Look!
I even force-feed my eyes:
a sky of sunflowers
is swelling heaps of gold.

AMBULANCE POEM

1

This is an ambulance poem. . . (I say
it importantly) My ventriloquist-
dummy and I start our daily dialogue.
He says Shut Up.
Familiar, contemptuous, we are
joint tenants of condemned property.
I call him Fool.

2

Poised on a diving board,
I rummage the ruthless
early swimming lessons.
"Over her head . . . she's over her head!"
My fool taunts and mimics a jig.
"See how her small hands paddle the air!"

Far below me,
The tank is a blue coffin
flanked by spectators
dawdling at cafe tables.
(Probably this is Juan-les-Pins)
Under striped awnings
they gawk and crane
flittering,
a fidget of leashes.
Behind my eyes
the ambulance
floats into focus . . .

3

That promontory of arrogant bones
composing a face weary of

itself even in the mirror:
the appointed rounds reduced
to a chair and the wait
for soup served
each day at twelve.
What are numbers
when each hour tilts
identically
at an ancient gifted woman
who has forgotten how to tell the time?
This woman is an exigency in space
past clocks past compass
and the stubborn set of North.

* * *

Inside the ambulance
a tearing of nightclothes:
from the sheets a blue hand
shoots out, cannot be warmed.
Into the acoustical traffic
of air-conditioned cars
the ambulance screams through keyholes.
Everyone is deaf.
The raucous scream
is a *magnificat*
for the dry shadows of clouds
laid over droughty mountains.
The ambulance rolls
to its own grand Recessional.

4

Most dangerous recess,
the pause next to last,
that mock-up of games:

Nail the runner
sink the bucket

smash the lob
finesse the Jack
crack the code
scale the summit
hunt the Grail.

And beat the clock beat the
clock beat the clock beat . . .

5

Now the celestial croupier!
Enigmatic collector.
Under a mirrored dome
he prances humming down the staircase
in white tie and golden tailcoat
a shimmer of cunning watch cases
swing from his cummerbund.
His sardonic falsetto
holds a feel for the pit
Faites vos jeux
Messieurs, Dames!
(Ritual pause.
Pragmatic smile.
Rake-hand flicks.)

And the random end?
A white-coated surgeon
twitching with a secret smile
leaves his emergency room early.
From the ambulance entrance
a trail of mirrors and knives,
the needles the thread.
Later he is
leapfrogging
over a quarry of sundials . . .
Sundials with no shadows,
freed from their prison of angles.

IV

HOUSE-DWELLER

No one had hit her before.
Not ever.

Now this stranger
with his cruel fists.
In her own front hall.
Her heavy glasses flying
over the silver vase,
over the red camellias.
A shatter against the cool redwood paneling.
All this clear, until
the terrible fists
closed her good eye,
and she fell to her knees
like a white circus horse
in a bulging red dream.
She knew the frailness of her own head.
Her navy jogging outfit,
a red wound slithering over the hardwood.

Why didn't he *take*
the TV and opera glasses,
jewlery cases,
the mounds and mounds of silver!
Scattered for flight by the front door.

Breath and blood fluttered
and broke from her mouth
instead of a scream.

She never knew the look of him.
Only a pulsing scar of a man
crazed with surprise.
The color of nightmare.

Early in the morning,
home from her solitary run
with salt sifting in her mouth,

she couldn't believe him.
Not at all, not inside
the heavy walls of her house.

Except for pain
he didn't exist.
He was only
a flick of wonder . . .
a hunch of fog riding in . . .
her own flinch at the edge of a cliff.

His blows sent her down
the drowning depth of a childhood lake.
A strangle of dying.

"His *color* the color of nightmare?"
The detective in the grey Justice office
was unable to fill out the form on his pad.

She whispered, "Yes.
"He left an icepick in the garden."
She thought of dahlias in gentle motion.

Then the giant policemen
said in a chorus,
"You'll be all right.
"He didn't take anything.
"You're alive, you know.

"You're lucky."

She said the word, then.
Ugly as dialect, it stumbled between
the stitched corners of her mouth:
"I want to go *home.*"

THAT TREE

Dust grits on the padded
knees of camels here
in the Beersheba market place.

North (I like the sound)
I will ride North.
To green orchards
in the Galilee,
greener than a shiek's emeralds.

* * *

And here I am . . .
The store-bought
wig of me unravels now
on a high gravel road
of mines and rusted tanks.
This choke of dust
falling over the rim
of my landscape
settles in layers
on a half-hinged door,
swung by the wind.

An Arab's dusty tree
stands alone in a front yard.
Black figs hang heavy as sleep.

Someone must water that tree.

SHARERS

(The Sixties)

This son starving himself before us
wishfully willfully
starving himself before us.
A son.

Meat growls in the oven,
red meat, steak meat best of show
and we know the taste of ashes.

He is the kin of animals
and fish and fowl
and roots.
The boy would be no cannibal.
Only fruit lying on the ground
may enter his bloodstream.
Even sugar cannot be boiled.
Its cells would moan through the stoveworks.

This son makes every room
in the house his showcase.
To the tunes of *ragas*
he reminds us of his mortality
as if that brief pause
were bronzed in a museum
poised in the shame of its flesh.

He faces east.

AT FIFTY IN THE CRYSTAL-DEAD EYE OF THE CENTER

A mare, my head cocking back
to see the meadow pass below,
I skin the trees at a canter,
hind feet skew out
to the soft cliff-edge.

At last a brittle beach,
and overhead,
swallows flanking swallows.
Oh, praise the Lord with rue!

Only the slide alone, now,
down the scoured sides
of sand dunes,
sifting on a wrist of wind.

CATHEDRAL

On Salisbury Plain
no rocks give.

Birds of the instant,
briefer than kinship,
dart from cloister to cedar,
the branches wide as a yielding giant.

Here the starlings
silence their wings,
let the racket
in their jealous throats
reel out
to the choir of boys
whose voices climb higher.
Higher than birds
wirespun to the sky.

These voices touch
granite alabaster marble
each stone colder than the last.
A hand can feel the difference.

My own hands trace the joints
where these rocks
will loosen
then skew and part.
Outlast *alone*
even records of their union.

SELLING OFF THE GARDEN

A deal's a deal,
that's gavel fair.
You gave your money,
we gave the deed
and never thought to cavil
with parenthetical clauses:

> *(You cannot subdivide*
> *the hiding place,*
> *the huge*
> *untidy laurel bush,*
> *safe as second-story hedges.*
>
> *Nor level off*
> *the terraces,*
> *trample out*
> *the berry brambles,*
> *strip*
> *the braiding palm leaves,*
> *uproot the tree-loft,*
> *then the tree.)*

Marooned now, that house
dumps a bony shadow, afternoons,
on the scraped lot next door.

AT LIBERTY

Snow lies in claws
on each plank of the porch.
Thin and fierce at the tips.

Preening, prodigal
in their brillance,
these crystals flex,
bend the light on the wind.
Prisms of a self
complete as a fly's eye,
they live off light,
give no heat.
Their harshness fixes us.

As our bodies curve in a frozen arc
toward them
(only our breath is warm)
their dazzle darkens.
They melt.

VIKING 1 ON MARS— JULY 20, 1976

1

What throws
this shadow of
the left-handed fencer
across the bright clubfoot
laid on Mars?

Our faceless, earthly
trespass
done in a plume of exhaust:
engines off
as the first leg
touches down.
No pilot clambers from the tripod;
no Martian runs across the ground.

Sunlight casts
long afternoon shadows
straight as the earth-crow flies.
Makes the same
skeletal selves we know.
The Martian swordsman,
left arm extended,
right akimbo,
is invisible.
Only his dark, grotesque image
reflects on the burglar's footpad.

Without life of its own,
(high-born on the food chain)
Mars radiates
its mythic warrior-spirit.
Full-blown it springs from
red boulders,

rusty craters
and the light, thin air.
Territoriality
is the spirit's shield.
For a saber,
it accretes
the strength of legends.

Calls on Zeus,
the father,
and on the sun
to twist the earthly spaceship
into cargo-shadows,
menacing as a
consortium of suicides.

2

Shadows shortcut
the Lander's superstructure.
Like black rafts
shooting rapids,
they bounce over
the froth of instruments;
carry truncated angles of
legs and switches,
shock absorbers and gauges,
seismometer and ground scoop;
a lop of the outsize, foreign ear.

This flux of shadows
flutters the edges of
struts and nuts and bolts
until the dark lines compose.
Until the imminent adversary forms.
This is the Martian defender,

grounded on the earthly footpad,
his shadow weightless as computer signals.

3

Oblivious of danger,
its orders stored a year ago,
the Lander's camera aims
a nodding mirror.

Across two hundred million miles,
on ninety million screens,
earth people watch
the image of Mars build,
computer-line by line.
The way children wait for the picture
in the jigsaw puzzle,
the dot-drawn coloring book,
the decal transfer.

We shed our thin
slipper of maxims.
Better than stolen fire,
better than Olympian secrets,
we forget the forfeits
for hubris:
the whole soup of early lessons.

We risk our geo-center,
risk a new Original Sin.
We dare to look:
to see the arc of
red dunes, dust and boulders,
the briliant sky of
another territory;
the ground unroll,

treeless, slow and sure
as a snake,
see it circle
the crewless freighter.

We know the Martian emblem,
already stamped on the Lander.
There will be no confrontation . . .
only the Seconds will fight the duel.

A new Bible begins.

IS THIS IT?

Is it the hollow of
birdbones? This
calling like a shrike
shrieking and knowing
no answer will come.

Or, this driftwood?
This sliver of driftwood
I hold in my hand,
silver as shavings of moon
wet in the harbor.
Its secret thinness, is this it?

Carnegie-Mellon Poetry

1975
The Living and the Dead, Ann Hayes
In the Face of Descent, T. Alan Broughton

1976
The Week the Dirigible Came, Jay Meek
Full of Lust and Good Usage, Stephen Dunn

1977
*How I Escaped from the Labyrinth and
    Other Poems*, Philip Dacey
The Lady from the Dark Green Hills, Jim Hall
For Luck: Poems 1962-1977, H. L. Van Brunt
By the Wreckmaster's Cottage, Paula Rankin

1978
New & Selected Poems, James Bertolino
The Sun Fetcher, Michael Dennis Browne
A Circus of Needs, Stephen Dunn
The Crowd Inside, Elizabeth Libbey

1979
Paying Back the Sea, Philip Dow
Swimmer in the Rain, Robert Wallace
Far From Home, T. Alan Broughton
The Room Where Summer Ends, Peter Cooley
No Ordinary World, Mekeel McBride

1980
*And the Man Who Was Traveling Never Got
    Home*, H. L. Van Brunt
Drawing on the Walls, Jay Meek
The Yellow House on the Corner, Rita Dove
The 8-Step Grapevine, Dara Wier
The Mating Reflex, Jim Hall

1981
A Little Faith, John Skoyles
Augers, Paula Rankin
Walking Home from the Icehouse, Vern Rutsala
Work and Love, Stephen Dunn
The Rote Walker, Mark Jarman
Morocco Journal, Richard Harteis
Songs of a Returning Soul, Elizabeth Libbey

1982
The Granary, Kim R. Stafford
Calling the Dead, C. G. Hanzlicek
Dreams Before Sleep, T. Alan Broughton
Sorting It Out, Anne S. Perlman